The Power of Purpose:
Living your Destiny

Michelle G. Cameron

THE POWER OF PURPOSE

Copyright © 2016 by Michelle G. Cameron
All rights reserved.

Published by:
NyreePress Literary Group
Fort Worth, TX 76161
1-800-972-3864
www.nyreepress.com

All rights reserved. No part of this book may be used or reproduced by any means, graphic, electronic, or mechanical, including photocopying, recording, taping or by any information storage retrieval system without the written permission of the publisher. Copying this book is both illegal and unethical.

Scripture quotations marked (KJV) are from the King James Version of the Holy-Bible. Copyright ©. All rights reserved.

"Scripture quotations taken from the New American Standard Bible®, Copyright © 1960, 1962, 1963, 1968, 1971, 1972, 1973, 1975, 1977, 1995 by The Lockman Foundation Used by permission." (www.Lockman.org)

ISBN print: 978-0-9972921-4-5
Library of Congress Control Number: pending

Christian Living / Inspirational

Printed in the United States of America

Contents

Reviews v
Foreword ix
Acknowledgements xi
Introduction xiii

Chapter 1: What is Purpose? What is Destiny? 1
Chapter 2: The Purpose of Purpose 3
Chapter 3: Starting the Journey 7
Chapter 4: The Practical Side of the Purpose Journey ... 11
Chapter 5: Barriers to Purpose 15
Chapter 6: Doors to Purpose 19
Chapter 7: Balancing Today with Tomorrow 23
Chapter 8: The Power of Purpose 27
Chapter 9: Living Your Destiny 29

Conclusion 31
About the Author 33
Contact Michelle G. Cameron 35

Reviews

Interested in discovering your purpose? Do you know the difference between purpose and destiny? Answering these questions and many more is Author, Michelle Cameron's new book, *The Power of Purpose: Living Your Destiny*. The book is penned with clarity and conciseness on the extremely important topics of purpose and destiny. In his national best seller, *The Purpose Driven Life* (Zondervan, 2002) Rick Warren tells us that life without a purpose is like motion without meaning. Cameron's book, written with passion, provides numerous opportunities for one to grasp purpose and experience a meaningful life. She points out how the power of purpose in our lives has the ability to empower and enrich the lives of many others.

Questions to answer and action items to complete gives *The Power of Purpose: Living Your Destiny*, a workbook feel. The reading and working on items designed to establish a clear picture of purpose is one of the many helpful aspects of the book.

There's no disappointment here. Whether it's for you personally, or you, the coach, you will be pleased with the clear sense of direction found in *The Power of Purpose: Living Your Destiny.*

Carole Dortch-Wright
Communications Executive
Dortch-Wright Enterprises, LLC

Michelle's book, *The Power of Purpose: Living Your Destiny,* was motivating, practical and spoke truth about life's journey. Without pursuing purpose, one can amble through life unfulfilled, and unable to help others around you that should be blessed by the manifestation of your passion on the path towards your destiny.

Nicole Cameron, MD

Dear Love, please sit down, grab your notebook and be prepared to tap into the recesses of your mind. You are now entering the Purpose and Destiny Zone. The purchase of this book has afforded you a one-on-one session with Michelle. Allow her passion to ignite your drive of discovery into the REAL you! You will quickly become focused and energized to step into the next level, as you either discover or re/assess your purpose and destiny! Is your job your passion, or do you need to rethink your goals? What seeds do YOU need to sow to achieve your destiny? Do not be fearful if your purpose exceeds your ability to complete it by yourself. That's precisely why you've picked up *The Power of Purpose*! A strategic plan fulfilled is equal to displayed results.

Belinda E. Oliver
Author
www.belindaeoliver.com

Passion. Vigor and Excitement. These are the first three adjectives that leapt out in my spirit after reading this much-needed unique resource regarding purpose and destiny. The author, Michelle G. Cameron, releases practical steps to engage us along our pursuit to finding our purpose in the earth. For years, we have all pursued destiny, but few people, unlike Cameron have ever told us our part in the process. Destiny is not achieved by sitting down, doing nothing, and waiting on it. Destiny is only achieved when we activate our faith and WORK! The Power of Purpose is a book for all purpose-seekers and destiny achievers.

Paul K. Ellis, Jr.
Author, *When Saints Pray & Transition: The Promising Distress*
CEO, Ellis & Ellis Consulting Group, LLC

The Power of Purpose: Living Your Destiny is a must-read for everyone who is seeking to fulfill his or her God-given purpose. Michelle Cameron challenges readers to discover their passion. Her practical guidance walks us step by step from purpose to execution. She reminds us that we have in us seeds of purpose to be watered and nurtured into a harvest of destiny. I firmly believe if we follow the advice given in The Power of Purpose, it will help us all make God's vision for our lives a reality.

> Dr. Matisa D. Wilbon, Associate Professor of Sociology and CEO of Matisa Wilbon Ministries

Foreword

Live past your grade school years and you start accumulating a short list of pressing questions to which you seek satisfactory answers. One of those questions is always some variation of, "Why am I really here?" Or "what purpose am I serving?"

In this book, Michelle G. Cameron goes right to the heart of the matter and addresses this question from a clear, this-is-how-it-works perspective.

This manual passionately serves as a step-by-step guide to finding your place in this world. Some books are entertaining and serve as great reads to pass time. But others, like this one, engage you on a treasure hunt and are like vaults where practical, valuable wisdom is stored.

This book will speak to areas of your life that have been in the dark for a while and will provide the necessary light for you to find your path on the way to a fulfilling life. Your life is about to change for the

Michelle G. Cameron

better. You hold the key to that change in your hands. Knowledge is power. Prepare to be empowered!

Hart Ramsey
Senior Pastor, Northview Christian Church
www.nccfamily.org

Acknowledgements

I am thankful to God for another opportunity to share my thoughts with you! I enjoyed writing this book, as I've walked this journey (and I am still en-route) in pursuit of my destiny.

I want to thank all who have supported my writings over the years, from my early blogging days on MySpace to this copy that you now hold. Thank you!

I am thankful for my family, especially my son who has watched me pursue my dreams as I've juggled other responsibilities while raising him. I pray that he will be blessed beyond measure as a result.

I am grateful for my friends who encourage me often. Thank you to all who believed in me by offering speaking invitations and buying copies of my other books. Special shout-out to Pastor Christopher Hutchinson, who believed in me from the very beginning! He invited me to my first major speaking engagement. I am very grateful.

Michelle G. Cameron

Thank you to my church family, Cathedral International; your continued support has been nothing short of incredible. I am honored to serve within such a wonderful ministry.

I am blessed, and forever grateful.

Introduction

For me, the journey to destiny and finding my purpose started early. I developed a love for reading from an early age. By the time I was ten years old I was reading classic literature written by the Bronte sisters (Wuthering Heights, Jane Eyre), Animal Farm (George Orwell), To Kill a Mockingbird (Harper Lee), and so on. My mom was a vocational high school English Literature teacher and a librarian, so books surrounded me all of my life. I started writing in my teens, and submitted writing samples to be printed nationally in Jamaica before I was sixteen.

As I fast-forward to today, I am thankful for my early discoveries. The application of what I loved took a lot longer than I had expected, but I am finally on the right track. Just know that the journey will be challenging, interesting, painful, and exhilarating, all at the same time – but don't ever give up! You will only get to do this once. Make the most of the time that you have here on earth and pursue your purpose.

Be determined to live out your destiny!

#TeamNoRegrets

Chapter 1

WHAT IS PURPOSE? WHAT IS DESTINY?

*J*ust about everyone is either speaking or writing about purpose and destiny nowadays, and with good reason. As we move towards the close of the 2nd decade in a new century, it seems fitting for all of us to seek and find our reason for existence. Some may just see this as meaningless rhetoric, but those who believe in God are convinced that we aren't accidents, and that we were born to live out a pattern, and walk on a specific path to fulfill a destiny before we leave.

So, What Is Purpose?

The *Merriam-Webster Online Dictionary* defines purpose as:
: *the reason why something is done or used : the aim or intention of something*
: *the feeling of being determined to do or achieve something*
: *the aim or goal of a person : what a person is trying to do, become, etc.*

Based on this definition, purpose pushes us to achieve specific goals, and it also helps us discover our reason "why" we're here.

Many of us have heard this famous quote: *"There are two great days in a person's life - the day we are born and the day we discover why (William Barclay)."* Without our "why" we won't see any reason to live meaningfully.

Now let's look at the word "Destiny."

Destiny is defined as:
: *what happens in the future : the things that someone or something will experience in the future*
: *something to which a person or thing is destined : fortune <wants to control his own destiny>*
: *a predetermined course of events often held to be an irresistible power or agency*

So, based on the definition here, destiny is the conclusion, or destination of purpose. When you discover your "why," your purpose-filled journey begins, which then leads you to your destiny.

I don't know about you, but just the definitions alone for purpose and destiny make me feel like throwing a party. I am excited to journey with you as you discover your why, and start your own progress towards what you will become.

So, let's start!

Chapter 2

The Purpose of Purpose

Much like I did, I am sure many of you are asking yourselves the following questions:

Why is finding my purpose important?

Why does it matter how I live my life, and what I do with my life?

Think of it this way: If no-one made an effort to pursue their purpose (or you may refer to it as a passion), we would wander aimlessly through life, miserable and unfulfilled. Many things would never happen. Think of the many inventions we enjoy today; someone had a passion or saw it as their life's purpose to invent useful items to enhance our lives. Think of many doctors, nurses, lawyers, and individuals who are in public office; many of them pursued purpose to be where they are today.

I often think of my youngest sister. Today, she is an accomplished pediatrician, a mom and wife. When she was only two years old, she plainly told us that she wanted to become a doctor. My family supported her from the moment she first articulated that desire; they bought her a doctor's kit. She went around taking our blood pressure and listening to our heartbeats for quite some time. We didn't doubt her ability to pursue her purpose. She excelled academically on every level, and at a young age we realized that she was highly intelligent and that her purpose was attainable. She finished high school with flying colors and was able to attend undergrad on a full four-year academic scholarship. After that, she attended medical school, also on a full scholarship. We watched her soar, as she got closer to what she desired all her life –becoming a doctor. It was no surprise to any of us when she graduated and moved on to internship and then to practice medicine. Her life was geared towards her purpose from a very young age, and she achieved it. She has other medically-related dreams, and I am waiting to see her implement those soon. Her purpose-filled destiny is now a reality that her family enjoys today.

Your passion in discovering your "why" fuels you as you wake up every morning. As you move towards your destiny, purpose allows you to see each challenge as a rung on a ladder; you are getting closer to your target.

Your purpose also becomes a map for your life; it orders your steps. In my previous example, my sister knew that she needed to work hard in school to accomplish her goal. It meant studying when she didn't feel like it. Sometimes her friends had fun without her. She had to push distractions away so she could finish what she set out to do.

With laser focus she checked off her purpose-filled milestones one by one, and with determination she accomplished a lofty goal with minimal debt. When you are on your path to purpose, you will also need to be on the lookout for ways to maximize your efforts and minimize loss, wasted time and squandered resources.

If you take a closer look at the lives of individuals who know why they are here and who are in hot pursuit of their purpose, they seem happier and fulfilled. Purpose fuels passion, and gives us that level of fulfillment that no ordinary job or career will do for us. That excitement is also very infectious and noticeable. We become inspired as we watch their purpose-filled journey and as they arrive at their destinies.

Here is the point: You are no different from them. You can reach your destiny too. And it doesn't matter how old (or how young) you are. Many of us are starting to realize that going along with the flow isn't as fulfilling as we once thought. It's important for you to know, that YOU KNOW, that you are on the right path for you. Following the crowd leads to dissatisfaction, emptiness and a depression that can follow you like a cloud everywhere you go. Many people feel so distraught that after a while, dying seems like a better idea. Just going to a good school for an excellent education and landing a dream job isn't enough. There's so much more to life than just pushing hard to make a lot of money.

The next chapter will give you some pointers to use as you determine where you are on your purpose journey.

Chapter 3

Starting the Journey

In 2015 I had the privilege of conducting a 3-session workshop with a group of singles at a local church. During our first session (which was quite an exciting time) we discussed some practical pointers in discovering our purpose. I am sharing it here with you as well.

Grab a pencil and a notebook, and let's go!

Think of three things that you LOVE to do; let's call it your LOVE TO DO list. These things are what you do now for free, or you would love to be able to do them all the time. Write them down.

After that, think of three things that irritate you. When you see it or hear about it, you are disgusted, angry or you want to help to make it right. You would do these things for free too, if given an opportunity. Write them down; this is your HATE TO SEE list.

Check your lists. Are you surprised by what you wrote? Or do they sound like something you knew about yourself for some time?

That list of six items has now become your "seed list" to guide you towards your purpose. For example, I love assisting people. I like sharing information that encourages and uplifts others. I have been that way for as far back as I can remember. I love to see others smile or watch them exhale a sigh of relief because of something I said or did for them, or with them, which helped them. This is one of the items on my LOVE TO DO list that has inspired me to write helpful books. It has pushed me to speak at workshops, conferences, and seminars as well. I believe I will continue to write because of this one item on my LOVE TO DO list.

Now that you've written your lists, how can any of these items be used every day or every week to enhance your life and the lives of those whom you will impact? Does it mean you need to return to school? Will you have to take some certification courses, or hire a coach/mentor? Will you need to volunteer someplace so you can begin to see the "nuts and bolts" behind your passion?

During one of the workshop sessions, I met a young lady, Ramona, who is a phlebotomist (and a very good one, from what I heard). A phlebotomist is someone who draws blood, and plays a key role in the medical field. But she also loves to do hair! She is currently in school for evangelism classes, as she has a passion to share the Good News with others, but she also loves these other things. She is now doing hair, but as I started taking careful note of how passionate she was about hair, I told her that I see her doing hair in her own salon. She currently drives all over (even to NYC) to clients' homes to give them fantastic hairdos. They would look like new people when she was finished with them. Trust me, I've seen the pictures!

Ramona was being referred by word of mouth as well. I asked her about it, and she felt conflicted because she also wants to become a nurse. I told her that since she is so young and has several passions, it should be possible for her to do all of them. We (because all the participants became involved) also suggested that she incorporate her passion for evangelism into her hair pursuits, as while she is making a woman look wonderful on the outside, she can share with her how to be restored spiritually through Jesus Christ on the inside. In that way, Ramona can combine her passions that are compatible. We also shared that she may be able to get hair clients as she does phlebotomy work, as they may ask who did her hair and she can proudly say she did it herself and, voila, a new client!

Her example may sound complicated to you, but sometimes, that's how purpose is displayed in some people's lives. It may be one main item, like my sister, or it may be multiple pursuits, like Ramona.

The list of six items you wrote is your "seed list" to review, pray over and research on how to use those gifts, talents and irritations into practical ways to enhance and enrich your life and the lives of others. Take note that our passions and purpose pursuits will never benefit just us. We are intended to help others along our life-journey, and our gifts, talents and passions are the tools that will enhance their lives and enrich ours.

Final Note: We have limited days here on earth. If you've lost a loved one, you know this all too well. So, let us step out and start the process of walking into purpose and begin moving towards our destiny.

Chapter 4

The Practical Side of the Purpose Journey

The purpose journey, on your way to destiny, is not an easy path to take. In fact, obstacles (as outlined throughout this book) may be plentiful. Here are some things you will need to do as you launch out into purpose. This list is generic, as everyone may need to pursue a different path.

1. Spend some time in prayer as you seek specific direction for your purpose.

2. Hire a mentor or a coach. This is an invaluable resource, as they literally shorten the timeline for you to get established. These are veterans; they know what you need to know, inside and out.

3. With the guidance of your mentor or coach, write out short-term and long-term plans for approaching and executing

your goals towards your life purpose. You may need to create an official business plan as well, depending on the type of scenario you will be navigating.

4. Get educated on what you plan to do or become. Take classes, or return to school for certifications or degrees as needed.

5. Find out what your legal requirements will be for your dream to become a reality. Legal counsel or the direction of someone who is established in something similar to what you want to do would be helpful here. Be aware of contracts, billing, refunding costs, etc., as this information will be highly valuable as you become established.

6. Register your domain name for websites or blogs. This helps you to secure your business, especially as it grows and matures. If you can, get all the versions: .com, .us, .org, etc. Don't be afraid to start off small and work your way to something spectacular. A WordPress website that can be managed on your own is a great way to get started until you can afford to invest in a web designer.

7. Register your business as an entity within your local state or country. Be prepared to pay taxes as you begin earning income on your dream. Be aware of local laws and requirements on operating your business – and comply.

8. Maintain certifications; renew business licenses or any other pertinent information as required.

9. Take out insurance; life insurance, health insurance, business insurance or any other coverage that will protect your earnings, just in case.

10. Save up for unexpected expenses as much as possible.

11. Create a plan that you can follow to get out of debt or to raise capital quickly if needed.

12. Consider long-term insurance, and prepare a power-of-attorney, a medical advance directive and a last will and testament.

13. Consider keeping a business lawyer on retainer, just in case.

14. Create vision plans for your business, and set goals each year, every five years, every ten years, etc. Review and revise them as needed.

15. For marketing, start small, and take advantage of free methods first. Consider printing business cards, and create an eye-catching logo that represents your brand. Trademark your logo.

16. Look for ways to offer free or discounted products and services to reviewers. They can share their thoughts on Yelp, or Amazon, etc.

17. Have your strongest supporters become your "testers" – where you can try out new concepts. This can be done via an email list for a newsletter.

18. Do what you need to do to create a strong, viable email list of clients and potential clients. These clients will get special announcements first, or special perks that general audiences do not experience.

19. Do regular check-ins with a peer support group who can offer great advice (many times based on personal experience). If you are interested in becoming part of a very vibrant group, I'm a member of a few good ones. Contact me (see my contact page at the end of this book) and I will invite you to one of them.

20. Only compete with yourself. Don't waste precious time imitating or coveting someone else's dream. Focus on building YOUR dream.

CHAPTER 5

BARRIERS TO PURPOSE

As you prepare to move ahead with pursuing your purpose towards destiny, you will meet barriers along the way. In fact, some of you will meet barriers from the start. This is actually quite normal.

Question: *What can hinder you from reaching your destiny or living out your purpose?*

Here are a few hurdles that several of us may have to climb over to reach our destination:

1. **Family and Friends** – They can discourage you from moving forward with your dreams with whatever reason they may offer to you. Although their reasons may be good, your prayer life and your faith in God will help you to continue pursuing your purpose. Just know that if God placed those desires within you, it will be important to remain obedient and

confident as you move forward. Be bold and push past the discouragement.

Scripture for Reflection: *"I can do all things through Christ which strengtheneth me." (Philippians 4:13)*

2. **Doubt** – You are hesitant on whether this is the right move to make. Ask God to remove your doubts as you pray. Ensure you've done all that you need to do to prepare for purpose. Taking tangible steps forward (like research, education, etc.) helps to minimize or remove doubt. **Scripture for Reflection:** *"Lord, I believe; help thou mine unbelief." (Mark 9:24b)*

3. **Fear** – You may be afraid because this is all new to you. You are now moving in a different direction, which may be outside of your comfort zone. Remember that if God is guiding you towards your purpose, He will provide for you and direct you as needed. Be prepared to lose friends, the support of loved ones and to be misunderstood by those who've known you. Don't allow your present circumstances to limit you. Tell fear to shut up, and be willing to step out. Be ready to do it afraid! **Scripture for Reflection:** *"Fear thou not; for I am with thee: be not dismayed; for I am thy God: I will strengthen thee; yea, I will help thee; yea, I will uphold thee with the right hand of my righteousness." (Isaiah 41:10)*

4. **Responsibilities/Obligations** – You may be a parent, or you may have a lot of expenses and feel that you must work many hours to cover your debts or obligations. You may be a caregiver for a loved one, and may feel that there isn't enough time to pursue your purpose. *Suggestion:* Set small goals that will get you started on the path to purpose. If you never start, you will never get there. As time goes by, as long as you have a solid plan on how to move closer to fulfilling your purpose, you will be able to find more and more time to dedicate to it. If there is an aspect of your purpose that you can monetize, you can start working on that part-time to help you cut back on working so hard otherwise. You will want to stop doing everything that will distract you from getting to where you need to be. If that means spending less time on social media, or less time going out with friends, or spending less money on eating out or shopping, then do so. Focus on what you need to do to get to where you need to go. **Scripture for Reflection:** *"Hear my cry, O God; attend unto my prayer. ²From the end of the earth will I cry unto thee, when my heart is overwhelmed: lead me to the rock that is higher than I." (Psalm 61:1 & 2)*

5. **Financial barriers** – Finances hinder many people from pursuing their purpose. This does not have to happen. Prepare a viable business plan and present it to organizations that are offering financial support to small businesses. Seek individual investors as well as banks or credit unions. There

may be companies that are seeking your services or skills; seek an audience with them so you can share your plan with them. Get guidance from individuals who may be connected to your purpose. These types of connections may exist in your local church, or among your relatives and friends. One thing is clear: Good character will open doors for you much faster than anything else. Be aware that investors will be looking for certain characteristics before they offer financial assistance – such as a strong work ethic, personal responsibility, reliability and evidence of strong financial management.

Another avenue towards financial freedom is blogging. Start an informative, eye-catching blog on a topic, or topics close to your heart, and as you grow your audience, you can approach compatible brands for marketing space on your blog. This is a viable source of income for many bloggers. **Scripture for Reflection:** *"But my God shall supply all your need according to his riches in glory by Christ Jesus." (Philippians 4:19)*

Can you add more to this list?

CHAPTER 6

DOORS TO PURPOSE

As you move towards your purpose, expect doors of opportunity and support to open as well! This is an exciting time for you.

Question: What, or who can push you towards your purpose?

1. **Family and Friends** – Some of us are blessed with family and friends who believe in us and in what we have to offer the world. You are in a wonderful situation if you are receiving support from those who are closest to you! **Scripture for Reflection:** *"In every thing give thanks: for this is the will of God in Christ Jesus concerning you." (1 Thessalonians 5:18)*

2. **Faith** – You have the faith to believe that once you step out, doors will open and opportunities will rise to meet you on your journey to purpose. Faith means stepping out when you

can't see the entire staircase or walkway. Take one step at a time and walk in it! **Scripture for Reflection:** *"Now faith is the substance of things hoped for, the evidence of things not seen." (Hebrews 11:1)*

3. **Determination/Hard Work** – As you get closer to your purpose, realize that this journey will take a lot of determination and hard work. Whether it's the work of laying the foundation for your business to flourish, or it is applying for certain permits, or returning to school for certain certifications or degrees, determination and hard work is needed to become and remain successful. Be prepared for long days and nights. You may encounter failures and setbacks. You may have to work two jobs: one during the day, and one when you get home as you prepare for your future. Whatever you need to do, roll those sleeves up and get ready to work! **Scripture for Reflection:** *"And whatsoever ye do, do it heartily, as to the Lord, and not unto men: [24] Knowing that of the Lord ye shall receive the reward of the inheritance: for ye serve the Lord Christ." (Colossians 3: 23 & 24)*

4. **Mentoring/Coaching** – As you navigate towards a new direction, you will need a coach or a mentor to guide you. Your coach or mentor should be already on the level that you are aspiring to be. This person will take the time to pour into you, based on their experience and level of success.

Prayerfully seek a wise person to offer guidance and nuggets on the journey. Be willing and ready to implement whatever they share with you; do not waste their time. Do not be hesitant to pay them if they require a payment. Make that investment in them and in yourself. Always show them the respect they deserve; they are human beings with shortcomings and flaws, just like you. Be careful not to hold their humanity against them. **Scripture for Reflection:** *"When I call to remembrance the unfeigned faith that is in thee, which dwelt first in thy grandmother Lois, and thy mother Eunice; and I am persuaded that in thee also. [6]Wherefore I put thee in remembrance that thou stir up the gift of God, which is in thee by the putting on of my hands." (2 Timothy 1:5 & 6)*

5. **Taking calculated risks** – We're excited about our purpose, and we're ready to walk into all that God has for us – our destiny. Before we start that journey, we prepare for it. Taking calculated risks means that we will do what is necessary to start working on our purpose, but we will not devastate or destroy our family or financial circumstances in the meantime. If we need to save up for a financial buffer while building the business, we do so. If we need to relocate for a better demographic of customers or clients, we will do so. If we need to raise capital quickly and we own valuable items, we're willing to sell them to pursue our purpose. We are willing to look at all viable options as we move towards

what God has called us to do. Pray for wisdom and guidance before taking action. **Scripture for Reflection:** *"For with God nothing shall be impossible." (Luke 1:37)*

Feel free to add to this list!

Chapter 7

Balancing Today with Tomorrow

In the previous chapter I mentioned stepping out in faith and taking calculated risks. As you move from where you are to where you need to be, you will begin to realize that this is a balancing act. You will discover that it may be easier to keep doing what you've been doing all along, versus transitioning from today's responsibilities and obligations into tomorrow's rewards. But they've said it, and you've heard it: nothing worthwhile comes easily.

I remember in the mid to late 2000's after my separation and divorce, with a toddler in tow, I decided it was time to go back to school. I started working on my MBA after working all day, every day. My son learned to amuse himself as I was stuck on my laptop every night completing assignments and reading material to answer questions or participate in discussions. During that time, I was introduced to MySpace. This was my first experience with social media. I was very hesitant, but after some time I became immersed in updating my profile and…. blogging. I've always been an avid writer, but many years had passed since I had put pen to paper. I decided to share some of my experiences. I basically used it as a type of journal (being strategically careful with how much I shared). As I wrote, I had no idea that people had started to find me and were reading my posts. Subsequently, they started contacting me to ask if I was going to write a book, and then it turned into, *"When are you going to write your book?"* After hearing that more times than I could count, I decided that it was now time to write. I completed my first book in 2010 and set it aside for almost one year. During early 2011, through a series of events I met and hired my first publisher. *It's My Life and I Live Here: One Woman's Story* was released in September 2011. I had tears in my eyes when I took home my first box of books and opened it. When the books were sold and distributed, I thought that was it.

The following year (2012) I graduated with my MBA, and during that same year I was asked to speak to some ladies in my country of origin, Jamaica. I flew down and shared my story with women from a wide age-range. Some ladies, who were old enough to be my mother, started crying silently as I spoke. They purchased copies of my books, and encouraged me. They hugged me like I was a long-lost friend. I was amazed. My books were now being sold and read overseas.

I returned to Jamaica in 2013 to speak for the first time on a Sunday morning to a congregation not far from where I spent my childhood. By the end of that session/sermon, several men and women came to the altar in tears. Some were crying and screaming. God moved mightily that day, and the pastor told me that I had a legitimate ministry and I should be open to what God wants to do. I must admit however, that I was very nervous when he said this to me.

By that time, I was already leading the Singles Ministry at my church in New Jersey. I felt honored to do so, and within one year of that appointment I completed preparation to become a licensed minister. During the time of leading the singles, I started to feel a burden for them. I kept meeting singles that were just drifting through life, or so it seemed to me. I started posting encouraging information that targeted singles on social media and gained a following that started asking…. *"Are you writing another book?"* So, in September 2014 I released, *I'm Single. Now What? 13 Steps on How to Live Single and Free.* This second book opened other doors; I started receiving speaking invitations for women's seminars, radio interviews and for a singles ministry at another church (multiple invitations from the same ministry). By now I realized that I was being ushered into another world altogether, doing things I would never have imagined me doing.

After the speaking engagements and book sales started, I realized that I had discovered my passion. I love helping and encouraging others, and I enjoy writing. I also rediscovered my passion for editing; this was something I did "for fun" years ago when my youngest sister was still in school. I edited her papers from middle school all the way until she graduated from her medical internship. Now I get to experience the excitement of new authors as they receive their edited manuscripts.

I was doing all of this while working in a corporate position that I did not enjoy. I had to find the energy to stay engaged, and only liked some of the tasks that I was assigned. Soon it was very apparent that my time of departure was at hand. I had very little control in the timing, but once I walked away I found a deep-seated peace that I had not experienced in a long time. My heart rested in knowing that I had the freedom to pursue my passions as desired. The leap of faith during this transition was no small matter.

I am still in a transition of sorts, as I do not know in detail what tomorrow may bring. But there is one thing I know that's certain; God has me in the hollow of His hand.

I've balanced today with tomorrow, and all shall be well.

Chapter 8

The Power of Purpose

*our Purpose Has Power.*

Did you know that?

Just like fuel for your car or a spark in an engine, purpose ignites you to move forward as you accomplish your goals. This "purpose fuel" also pushes you as new opportunities and doors open for you. As you walk into your purpose, your life starts a powerful chain reaction in the lives of others. This means others on social media, your family members, friends, church associates, coworkers and clients, and the list goes on. Your boldness to step out into the unknown will cause others to re-evaluate their life choices and may inspire them to take the plunge as well.

What supplies your purpose with fuel? Your passion unleashes the "power fuel" of purpose. It also diminishes and extinguishes the power that others may try to hold over you. When you are fully engaged in your purpose, no boss, coworker, parent, demon – nothing or no-one – can keep you down or stop you. Sometimes roadblocks may appear, and this is quite normal, but you will get the wisdom, energy and power to tunnel through them. Wisdom may come in the form of a support group, or a friend, a fantastic book, a Scripture verse or the lyrics to an uplifting song. Look for genuine support and encouragement when you feel like walking away or giving up – because you will get to that point sometimes. Also, be willing to offer that same level of support to others who are on the purpose journey with you.

The power of purpose boosts you to keep going even with few (or no) supporters – at least for a short time. If you notice that when a car has a full tank of gas, it doesn't need any coaxing to move ahead. As long as the engine is working as it should, the car will drive. In the same way, as long as we are connected to our passion, and we have worked on our spiritual, emotional, mental and physical aspects, our purpose will move ahead. "Purpose fuel" propels your dream forward.

Note that you will need to refuel for your purpose journey from time to time with retreats, rest, conferences, and revisiting your overall vision or plan. Again I will emphasize the need for leaning on a strong support team or group that will help you refuel.

With great resources, such as great conferences, books, retreats, a mentor/coach, etc., and a powerful network you will begin to soar higher than you could ever imagine.

Don't limit yourself. Keep moving forward!

Chapter 9

Living Your Destiny

s you unleash the power of purpose, you begin to live out your destiny. Be open to where it takes you, as you go to places and meet people that you never imagined.

I've learned that sometimes we limit our journey to destiny and ourselves because we're aware of the increased demands that others will place on us as we become more experienced and proficient at what we do. To live out our destiny at the highest level, we must prepare our minds, bodies, and spirit for more, for higher, and for greater.

When the doors of opportunity open (because they will), step through them with your head held high. Prepare for huge opportunities in advance. Be diligent. Your gifts will make room for you and bring you before great men! (Proverbs 18:16, NASB) To stay in the presence of these great men, you must be able to deliver quality, stellar service or products every time. You must develop a system or process that will help you deliver high quality service or products every time you make contact with your clients. Your future and your continued success will demand it.

Let us leave mediocrity behind, and let us move towards more, higher and greater! Let's live out our destiny!

Conclusion

It's my hope that this book has encouraged and inspired you as you start your pursuit of purpose towards your destiny. You are now part of a great group of people who are tired of merely existing, and who desire to live vibrant, meaningful lives while inspiring others to do the same. We want to use all the gifts, talents and skills we possess in the ways that God desires us to use them. We want to die empty. Myles Munroe once said, *"Don't die old, die empty. That's the goal of life. Go to the cemetery and disappoint the graveyard."*

Note that as time passes, the path to destiny may seem to change; what most likely has happened is you've entered a different season on the journey. Where you were once the student, you have now become the teacher or mentor. Where you were an apprentice, you're now considered the expert; people now seek you for wise advice and counsel.

Stay focused. Pray. Read. Study. Learn. Process, and Execute!

I'm cheering for YOU!

About the Author

Michelle Cameron is an avid writer since the age of 15 with recent features on the "Black and Married with Kids" website. She released her first book, *It's My Life and I Live Here: One Woman's Story* in 2011. Michelle's second book, *I'm Single. Now What? 13 Steps on How to Live Single and Free* was released by NyreePress on September 12, 2014. Her first book "It's My Life" was re-released by NyreePress also in 2014. Her third book, "Write That Book! The New Author's Success Guide" was released in September 2015 as an e-guide.

Michelle is passionate about helping others pursue and realize their dreams, so now she edits books to help new authors share their stories with the world.

As a former Toastmaster, Michelle is honing the art of public speaking, and uses blogging and social media outlets to inspire and uplift men and women with her testimony. Michelle is a licensed minister at Cathedral International in New Jersey and is the mother of one son.

Contact
Michelle G. Cameron

Website: www.michellegcameron.com
Blog: www.michellegcameronwrites.com
Twitter: https://twitter.com/ShellyLove2002
Instagram: http://instagram.com/shellylove2002
Facebook: https://www.facebook.com/MichelleGCameronLLC
LinkedIn: Michelle G. Cameron
Email: michellegcameron@gmail.com
Mail: P.O. Box 1693, Piscataway NJ 08855-1693

Other titles from the Author: *It's My Life and I Live Here: One Woman's Story* (Godzchild Publications, 2011; NyreePress Literary Group, 2014).

I'm Single. Now What? 13 Steps on How to Live Single and Free (NyreePress Literary Group, 2014).

Available in eBook format everywhere eBooks are sold.

Michelle G. Cameron is available for speaking engagements, individual or group coaching/consultations, writing workshops, book editing and assisting singles ministries everywhere as requested. Please contact her (*michellegcameron@gmail.com*) for details and references.

www.ingramcontent.com/pod-product-compliance
Lightning Source LLC
Chambersburg PA
CBHW040336300426
44113CB00021B/2766